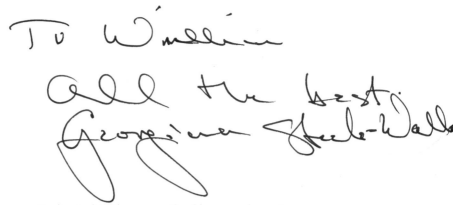

To William

All the best.

Georgina Steele-Walls

Dedicated to the strength of human character

D1235562

...AS I WAS SAYING...

A continuation of "In My Life, So Far..."

APRIL 1, 2018

If you haven't read "In My Life, So far..." this is a summation of events since the penning of that memoir and a continuation of life.

FORWARD

I have been inundated with queries and requests to either write another book, a continuation of my memoir, or something along similar lines. A sequel of sorts to "In my Life, So Far…"

I had only things to add that have happened subsequently, like the death of my horse, Sun. I now have had the first real encounter with my now ex-husband, Gordon, more insight into what I escaped from by letting him go and so forth. I am fortunate.

I shall begin this around the time of where I left off. I was getting used to the fact that Gordon was not what he seemed, and sometimes more than what he seemed on the surface. Hindsight is 20/20, and it just keeps coming up and slapping you upside your head on a regular basis once you get your thinking in some sort of pattern.

When I completed the first book I was in a rush to finish it and get it out there, after about twelve years of adding to it and changing it around, the exit of Gordon that warm

November afternoon in 2006 catapulted me into a fever of writing and compiling of photos and events to end that chapter in my life, or at least express myself with a view to having to do that.

The odd thing about it is that as soon as I wrote it down, everything ended. The dedication alone, "to Sun and to Gordon", named who was leaving, but I didn't know it was "The End".

****

The pleading and begging to come home faded away into an obscure thought. I immersed myself once again in the life I have always lived, before Gordon, during Gordon, and after him as well. The unexpected series of events that snow-balled to the present is mind-boggling to say the least. One thing after another, changing my direction and my perception, and my life.

I did not go easily into it, nor am I completely in acceptance of it all. Depression takes time to dissipate, or get used to at least. 'Deal with it', is all I could tell myself. Fortunately my friends were there if needed, and knew to keep distance when they weren't required to take any action with me. I went as low as I think I could go, and live. I was constantly chiding myself into 'getting over it'.

It wasn't the dissolution of my marriage that caused all of these emotions, not directly, and I won't give too much credit to my ex for my condition. We had almost broken up long before we separated, no one had the guts and

3

gumption to take that first step outside of our relationship. It just happened, another strange series of events.

Gordon went on tour, he didn't return, I was shocked and then uncertain. Then a mad and murderous feeling consumed my waking hours. I threw it off and immersed myself in my writing and the care of my horse, my house, and other animals. Oh, and myself.
I re-found my place in my own space, I had been moved aside as a wife and didn't like the relegation. I had to find my self-worth again. It had been systematically stripped from me along with my pride and motivating forces necessary to be a person in my own right.

There was one other descent upon me by the Gordon faction, in March of 2007.
He descended upon me one morning, preceded by a Glendale policeman (to see if I was armed and dangerous), who knows the tales of woe that must have been spun by my spouse. He arrived with an army of his O Gauge train buddies and Ray, whom he had run over on that last day here; Having run out of booze, a very drunk Gordon decided to make a run to the liquor store, Ray managed to catch him and reached in the window to take the keys out of the ignition, Gordon floored it and Ray was thrown across the road with a few broken ribs and a fractured pelvis, he wouldn't report it as he wanted Gordon to like and trust him.
He also brought, not one, but two body-guards, I assume to keep me away from him.

4

It was pitiful, he mumbling and shaking and weeping as he directed his 'minions' to take this or that, averting his eyes in either fear or shame, I never found out.
They swept through the house stripping every item even holding a vague association with masculinity. I, therefore became devoid of all tools and such.
Into the huge U-Haul they went, off into the night.

Well, not quite. I don't let go that easily when I have been blindsided and bamboozled!

Off the body-guard went with Gordon in one car and Ray drove the U-Haul. I followed a twisting turning trying-to-lose-me drive. Finally, Ray pulled into the police station parking lot to shake me off once and for all. I gave up after a bit of trying to chide Ray into telling me where Gordon went. I got tired of the duplicity and went home.

As I said, that was the end of March of 2007. April and May were getting better. I moved Sun to a new facility, affordable and nice and planned on doing a few upgrades to secure the premises. Toward the end of May, a beautiful evening, walking my dog Caesar I ran into a neighbour out walking her dog Rebel, we got to talking and before I knew it my little Caesar went after a rabbit or something and I was pulled off my sandals and onto my left hip!

Now, as those who know me and have read the first book, I have had both my hips replaced, you are not ever supposed to fall on these new prosthesis, but there I was

5

lying on the street, afraid to move. I got helped home and subsequently to the ER. I had fractured my femur in the Greater Trochanter area at the top, the hip joint was fine, but I was on crutches, being admonished not to put my weight on it. Sure.

My friend Don Adey had come to take me to the ER and before we did so we went and fed Sun and cleaned his stall, always first in my priorities. But what would I do for 6 to 8 weeks?
As usual I managed to get there twice a day, taking Harvey to help with the heavy lifting, and Karen and her husband Forrest came and walked him around the block most nights.
We'd get through this. Or so I thought.
Fate has a cruel way of stepping in and putting up barriers to let us know what we can or can't do. I hate it!

Chapter II

The new enclosure Sun was in was good solid concrete on two sides, with a gate at one end and a pipe fence down the other side length. I had noticed he had been rolling in a spot too close to the pipes for comfort, with his propensity for casting, rolling and getting their feet stuck up on a wall.

I intended to put up boards for a safety barrier, just as soon as I could get off these crutches.
I rue the day I didn't get someone else to do it.

I was awoken at about 6AM on the morning of the 15th June 2007. It was Jerry, the owner of the house I boarded Sun at the back of, in Burbank, CA.

When Jerry had awoken he found Sun lying trapped under the pipe fence, it looked bad.

I raced over there, only about three miles, he was up on his feet but very traumatized and shaky. He had lain there for how many hours I can only guess, on an uneven flooring with a board wedged under his left foreleg. I called the vet and after what seemed like forever he arrived and gave him some Bute and other medications. He went away and I stayed. Sun was so in shock that he lay down with me and groaned, the vet returned later in the day and then still later, about 5pm, to say he thought I had better get him to an equine hospital quickly, he was urinating blood. His creatinine levels were too high. I ran across the street to Sheila's, she has a trailer, she hooked it up and we were on the road to Chino Equine Hospital, about 50 miles east of here, on the freeway, on Friday evening.

When we got him there they examined him and didn't like his condition. I began a long vigil that would last some 6 ½ weeks and cost way over $14,500. I couldn't lose my boy, not after only twenty-two years.

I knew my horse, these vets didn't. I am sure they are wonderful practitioners but I knew my Sun.

After about two days he seemed to rally. The swelling in his leg was draining and they wrapped him, his appetite was good and his urine running clear. I wanted to bring him home. The vet told me he needed to keep him longer. I should have brought him back. The accident and stress was too much, he needed to be in familiar surroundings again. I should have checked him out and brought him home, but believing the powers-that-be I let him stay a few days more, then the worst news on my arrival one day, I went daily and stayed till they threw me out at 8PM, he had foundered! Laminitis, the dreaded crippling condition that took Secretariat, Barbaro and many others.

It is a condition where the tiny laminae inside the hoof wall die and the coffin bone, centre of the hoof separates from the hoof wall, rotating and sinking. Their feet for all intents and purposes 'fall away'.

The dreaded stretching out stance to relieve the pressure on the front legs is a sure sign.

The dreaded Laminitis stance

Still I hoped for the condition to stop in its' tracks, as it sometimes will. He got worse and worse. I couldn't do the deed as he was eating and on a drip for water, a tube descending from a supply of water, through his nose to his stomach; I could get him to drink from the bucket I held for him. I lay with him all day and night and wouldn't have eaten if it hadn't have been for Bill and Carole Wenda, nurses who live in the Chino area, coming to take me out to eat nightly. They were very kind to me.

This consumed me, I was frantic.

Daily I would get a call from the hospital telling me the additions to my bill, "put it on the credit card" is all I would say.

Finally I could take no more tension, traveling and expense and there was a hauler there I hired to bring Sun and I back to Burbank.

My wonderful horse seemed to understand and walked sprightly to the trailer and stood the entire trip back, he was walking fine as he re-entered his stall area, I thought it had turned around. But that is about all Sun could do, turn around a few times and then he lay down. I don't believe he was able to stand again, not for a few days and then only because of what the vet gave him.

I have expressed this story again and again, out loud, and nightly in my head. I stayed with him, he had a fever now and I sponged him off on a regular basis and when I couldn't Mara and her son Andreas stood the vigil.

Finally the vet told me I had to make a decision. She could 'keep him alive' for about $2000 a week, or we could do the right thing, as Sun was now in too much pain.

Sun's last day

I steeled myself for the following day, July 23rd 2007.

My friends, Gail, and her little doggie Gracie came up from San Diego, Cathleen came from work and Keith Allison came to sit and watch with me. Cindi Woods, an animal communicator came and told me things only Sun would have known, told me what he loved and what he wanted and to look out for him in May as he would try to come back to me. Great hopes and dreams.

Fortunately for me there were other matters the vet had to attend to and 2PM became almost midnight before she arrived. I was a basket case, lying with him, sponging him off and crying. My wonderful friends let me do it my way.

Finally the vet gave him a shot of something that would allow him to rise once more to go into the alley behind and have the deed done.

The renderers were sitting patiently some ways off ready to dispose of his earthly remains. He was going back to the earth. My life

The actual medical things that followed will haunt me for the rest of my life, I sit here crying as I write, now some 9 months later. He stood proud and only fell to the ground for the final shot when tranquilized into it. I was lying across his neck and we whispered our good-byes.

I can't go on about it, I went back to retrieve his things a few weeks later, but not at once.

****

I couldn't do anything, breathing was getting to be too much. I sought help with a therapist and got some meds to ensure I could continue breathing.
My friend Suzie called me from Cabo San Lucas and invited me to get away. I had enough miles to pay for it, so departed for Baja, Mexico and rode horses on the beach every night, trying to make sense of it all.

Riding 'Gasparine' in Cabo San Lucas

After about ten days I returned to find divorce papers, initiated by Gordon, in the mailbox. He had had me served while all this was going on. He had moved to Nevada to expedite the process.

I really couldn't deal with it, I had lost everything and it looked like the house would be next. I cowered here at home, crying, raging against everything and everyone. What could anyone do to me that could be worse than what I had just been put through?

Somewhere inside us is a marvelous thing. Call it the instinct to survive or what you will. Your mind will not let your body die, not easily. You can't just fade away. Some fickle finger of fate steps in and just makes you do the

13

things it takes to make it through. Some call it God, others, the universe, I call it self-preservation, and it was strange.

Suddenly it seems that from everywhere at once there are opportunities to take, that you have to take an option on, at least.
Like floundering up from the depths of the ocean just before your air gives out.

No one actually came to me and told me I had to get it together. I am sure I was being worried about, but I was left to do it myself. The things I needed were inside me, I had to take hold and work with myself. Work with the forces that were there around me and inside of me.

Finances being the utmost concern and the state of living was next. I had to get some repairs done on this house, even though I felt I would lose it due to the enormous debts I had incurred. There are options and I took them and took that weight off and am still learning what I can do to maintain my peace of mind.
New copper pipes, new windows, fixed my teeth and took better care of myself. Ate again.
The power of life is really amazing. Too many people give up, I know I thought that would be preferable to living a life without Sun, without family without a husband.
Now I seem to have re-found myself, I got covered up during my marriage, I became an extension instead of the separate entity I had always been.

It is still, I am still, a work in progress.
There are fabulous things to believe in and a lot has to do
with friends putting these strengths in my way, to pick up
on, or fall over as-it-were.

My faith is negligible. I deal in practicalities and logic. I
suppose I am spiritual to my environment, in-other-words, I
am aware of my surroundings and my place on this planet,
as a part of all the elements and organisms we share. I see
the reality and know no one is responsible for my condition
but myself, begging for help, or as some say 'praying', is a
futile waste of time. I think the last time I even tried praying
was for Sun. He didn't improve, things seemed to be
conspiring to do just the opposite of what I prayed for.
The only change we, as humans, can achieve is by our
own actions.
 It is a challenge, sure, but it is certainly more rewarding
when you get what you need to be accomplished. My way
seems to make me go into a more positive frame of mind
so that the good can surmount the bad energies and rid me
of self-imposed repression.
"There are more things in heaven and earth Horatio, than
are dreamt of in our philosophies" holds more truth than
you may know. Too many just pray and with no positive
results, they give up, abandon all, including their own lives.

****

Recently, one of the friends from the old days decided it
wasn't working for him and took his own life. Randy wasn't

impulsive even in this, that he planned out every detail to withdraw his own way. It really sucks to leave so many with questions, that now you find you don't have the means to comfort others with answers, doesn't it my friend? My question to you would be, why in the hell did you file your Income Taxes?

Gail Murphy with Randy Gannon

Another, closer friend, J.P., John Pitre, my old friend with benefits for a while during the Forge days of the 1980's couldn't face the unknown either. So sad. John's wife, Annette had died of lung cancer not long after discovering she had it. JP was desolate and lost, he would call and ask me how to get through it. "Live" is all I could tell him. He sought help by attending some Evangelical Christian cult, 'grief' meetings and there he met a woman who sounds like she was just trolling looking for a wealthy widower. The vulnerable JP married her. I know not what occurred in their brief relationship, but a mere 3 months later, I got a call that he was found in his garage with what appeared to be a self-inflicted gunshot wound to the head. Just the location of the wound seemed highly suspicious as it was in the rear of his head…so sad, such a waste, and possibly criminal.

That is why, when we have a reasonable amount of health and ways to make it better, we shouldn't give in to depression and defeat. Sure, it is easy to lose all control over your life, by dulling your senses. True, you won't hurt anymore for those reasons, but you get a whole set of new problems. Why compound matters? Or worse, giving up altogether, this only removes you from the world, you don't go to an easier or better existence. The religions, in my humble opinion, have no right to delude vulnerable people with the thought that they will see their loved one's again when they die, too many can't wait. Sort of like being a suicide bomber to get the 72 virgins!

****

It would have been preferable to not have to deal with all the drama and tragedy of losing Sun, and other losses and defeats, but what sense is there in that? You get over the loss, or at least you get used to it. To be so very lost and desolate that you can see no future is something to be dealt with, for if you follow those impulsive desires, you are being selfish to those friends your leave behind to deal with your senseless loss. What is it people always seem to say when someone takes their own life? "If only they had said something!" Well, I suppose that goes for the both of you. Be aware without being intrusive.

19

Through self-analyzing, and introspection, and sometimes just saying what you are feeling out loud, no one will judge, and if they do, you don't need those kinds of people in your life.

This toying on the fringes of therapy is an interesting experience. Always the pragmatist I cut out a lot of sessions by just giving the psychiatrist a copy of my memoir to read. So much easier!

Now that I have my life returning to me, and much more together than it was before, I have had the experiences of my marriage and other things in my life, I find a whole new optimism and self-confidence. Plans for the future, my future, make themselves apparent constantly.
  I find a settling of sorts that makes all that struggling and searching I did the first half of my life become much more plain, and easy to understand why and how it all has happened.

I feel more accomplished, not trying to prove something or to get approbation from someone else. It feels safer and surer; as I feel I have hit bottom with my feelings and there is nowhere to go but either up, or stay on an even keel, dealing as I go along. In order to do this, I now find I have had to shut down somewhat in some areas, in order to gain strength from other areas of my life.

It was a hard lesson to learn and my denial about the passing of time and those in it, well it is wearing away somewhat.

I had fears, fears of losing what I was familiar with, what I loved. But they all pale with the big ones, the loss of parents, friends, my finances and then the biggest, to me~ Sun. Now that they are lost to my every day, I realise we all have our times together, when they're gone, nothing can be done but remember them fondly.

Now with other personal tragedies, I seem to not get too involved emotionally anymore. I am sad and anxious for a bit, then deal with the details and move along. For nothing can hit me quite that badly again. Now when the phone rings at odd hours I don't panic as I always had a tendency to do before, what with a mother in her 90s in the U.K. and a horse who would pull something that needed to be dealt with at all hours.

As I have said, Sun was a pivotal time in my life. I bought him instead of buying cocaine, He took that spot and let it grow into a beautiful relationship, and no one could destroy it. For twenty-two years, from the time he was two years old till the day he had to go away and re-group as he seemed to think he was doing, according to the psychic. We shall see how he thought it out, throughout all those years and times, it was Sun whom I went to when troubled or sad, he would come over and gently put his head in my lap. The love and responsibility I felt for that horse kept me continuing to be a productive and responsible person. My duties, always a pleasure, usurped anything else that came along in my life to do. I am somewhat lost with all this time on my hands now. Like I am failing at something, like there is something to do, but there isn't, nothing pressing any more. I can live at leisure to some extent. I miss his presence daily. No other horse holds the same feeling for me. I have only just recently been able to go into the Rancho district of Burbank again. I took my friends Jill, who was visiting from back East, to see where it all happened, visited at the Equestrian Centre was spotted by a couple of horses and a burro I used to know and was fawned over, chewed on and nudged. It felt good, it was also wistful for me as I couldn't go get on Sun and ride around these same places. But I made strides in that I was even able to go into the neighborhoods where I rode on my steed for over twenty two years, and hoped to continue, had an expectation of continuing for at least another ten or fifteen years. We were supposed to ride into the sunset together.

****

All through the times of the accident with my femur, Sun's accident and subsequent demise I never heard a word from my ex-husband, well we were still married actually, I ignored the papers and never signed them. But no, not a word, not even indirectly. I always knew he was selfish and self-serving, but that is just cold.

Roughly a year to the day after he last descended upon me at the house, he called again. I have been waiting for him to collect the rest of his things and finally he arrived the beginning of April 2008. With a rental car, too small for the job he poked about prying his train track up, leaving the platforms for me to deal with, when the car was full he left again. The negative energy in the house was cut-table with a butter knife. I had to burn sage in every space to cleanse out the remnants of what he left behind. He says he will have to make another trip, says he is married again.

Of course he did this the following day, by phone, from the safe distance of Vegas. Very fuzzy on the details so I think the alcohol was guiding his tongue toward the hurtful mode. Or so he thought, I don't feel hurt, his life is now his own and the poor sods who have to deal with him.

I am not saying I still didn't want to love him, at a distance though. I treasure the memories I have of our first meeting and other subsequent 'firsts' for me.

He will not see the errors he is making and I think he is actually alone with his misery once again. For even with others around, Gordon was so very alone.

He calls, tries to assert himself again, but he is too late. I tried to find some common ground, some semblance of what Gordon once was. Not a thing. Not in looks, nor in personality or charm, no it had all gone, or was being hidden. Just misery and debasement and a false sense of self-importance in the scheme of things. He commiserated about Sun, of that I feel he had genuine sorrow. But the same old sleights and digs were inserted into his conversation with skill. He goaded me into arguing, and I fell for it for a while, then realized, I don't have to any more.

I did tell him that we have been friends for over 45 years and with all our history together it would be a shame to let a bad marriage ruin it all. He seems unsure as to whether he wants peace and understanding or if he wants to continue his dramas and imagined hurts.

It is sad to see someone go away so thoroughly yet still be very much in the fore-front.

He tells me he didn't read my first book nor see any interviews on me, hard to admit, for him, that someone else has actually accomplished something with their life. He again relies on the tell-tales of friends and sycophants to tell him things. He thinks I slagged him off in the last chapter of my book. Far from it. I still foolishly hoped he would come back one day, at that time. I was most generous to him and his ways in "In my life, So Far…".

I find it hard to believe he didn't peek in the book just to find passages about him. Strange. I spelt his name right, which is the important thing they say. Whoever 'they' are! It proved to be another catalyst into my writing so I thank him for that. I have been in a sort of limbo not knowing what his plans were with regard to things he left here at the house. At least he has his clothes and books now.

It is an odd state of affairs. He is off on a tour back east so I am sure that chapter has more insights coming.

****

*I have had a lot of feedback from the first book, from friends, and just readers.

There is more?

Yes, there is more.

In my haste to get the book finished I forgot a lot of incidents, segues into other stories and so forth. I shall have to now recall what they have all been I suppose.

Memories are for remembering after all.

I must say your interest warms my heart!

****

I have just completed my stay at the Time Share in Carlsbad, CA. May 2008.

Way back when, in about 1996 Gordon and I went on one of those free week-ends, if you go to the presentation seminar offers.

Somehow we thought it a good deal at the time and I wrote a cheque. It is for every other year and we always went together. Till the last couple of times anyway.

The past two holidays Gordon got himself arrested for pushing his elbow into my ribs when I tried to keep him from falling over from drinking, he had to go somewhere! I mean he couldn't stay at the house, not with Karole watching the animals, he had thrown her out bodily one time before. He certainly was in no shape to accompany me down to the condo so off he went, he got out after the week end and the police had enforced their own TRO (Temporary Restraining Order), so he stayed at Bob Colbert's out at Malibu and when the week restriction was

25

gone, and he was sober, he joined me for the last day of the trip. He was awkward and uncomfortable while remaining obstinate and argumentative.

The time after that, he had a gig in Tennessee so we went down there, and he flew off to Jackson from San Diego, when he returned we stayed on a few more days and that was OK. He had gotten so out of it in Tennessee he left all his stuff there. So he lessened his intake those few days. But, this is not to chastise Gordon for past indiscretions, he does that for himself often enough.

While Gordon was off in Tennessee I thought to call my dear friend Arthur Lee. He had been diagnosed with Leukemia and was in hospital in Memphis. We talked for quite a long time. Arthur said he was going to beat this, I offered my bone marrow, but, having had Hepatitis C it wasn't allowed. He joked how he would rather have Hep. C than Leukemia. He said he would be back in L.A. in August, to continue touring with Love, he was back in August all right, but it was in a box. The leukemia took him out while Gordon and I were in Chicago for the Beatlefest. Rest in Peace dear Arthur. You are missed.

This time the trip was different, this time I went alone; not having him there or joining me was odd sometimes; when you do something recurrent after a break-up I guess that is the way of things, but strange it was. Pleasant, uneventful, relaxing.

My friend Lizzie Banks, who lives in Carlsbad, and I had a
few good adventures around the San Diego area, did some
shopping and 'girl' things. Mango Mojito's in Old Town San
Diego. It was a good time for a change.
I decided to attend my 43rd High School reunion for
Hollywood Professional School the following month and
found the perfect dress and shoes in a boutique in La Jolla.

My 43rd high school reunion Sportsman's Lodge, Studio City 2008

The reunion the following month was interesting; I remembered no one at all really. My time at school wasn't particularly memorable and I didn't hang with any of my classmates at the time, but as I had become re-acquainted with some of the alumni since My Space and Facebook had put us all in touch, so I decided to go.

No sooner had I entered the Sportsman's Lodge in Studio City and gone up to the bar but this man came up and said hello. Bob Granite had been at HPS, I suppose, at the same time I was, I was only there from 1965 to 1967, and absent a lot. Bob tells me his mother had been my mother's theatrical agent for a while, and I sort of remembered. He and his lady Lily, a nice Chinese woman seemed pleasant enough. I invited them and Jodie Carn and a few of the HPS crowd to Thanksgiving that year, 2007. They would invite me to various events, I usually declined, and they had a place at the Castle Green in Pasadena and seemed to do a lot of import/export between China and the USA. I went to a few events at the Hotel, garden parties and so forth. Just another re-acquaintance. More on this later.

****

I have started to come out of my self-imposed restrictions of behaviour. Weird that I should have found myself bound by anything more than respect and love I had for my husband and marriage vows, but I feel, still, like I have to ask permission and approval for my actions. This is a negative part of relationships I think. To be too free seems careless and to conform is so restricting.

29

Perhaps I just never developed in that area of emotions, but it is too stressful to contemplate changing now.
Some people are never meant to be bound by the constant presence of others.
I, personally find it too confining, at least with most of the relationships I have had. To always be aware that my actions are affecting someone in my immediate surroundings, always seeking approval or approbation.
I suppose being an only child had a lot to do with my developing this way. I am remembering now, after Gordon has been gone for a couple of years, that I had a full and content life before I acquired another 'half', and can have a full and content life again. If that is what the Universe holds for me.

'There are the kore; women-who-will-never-marry, in the folklore of many cultures.
This aspect of the female psyche wishes to keep to herself alone. This is mystical and solitary in a good way, for the kore is taken up with the sorting and weaving of ideas, thoughts, and endeavors.

I often feel this is where I lean; a self-contained wilder woman that is most injured by trauma or keeping a secret of others, the peace and presence of mind I seek is usually only attainable when in my solitude, I have then, the integral sense of self that needs not much around to make me happy. In my own environment I can weave my life on the loom and be at peace.

No matter how often I have been injured and killed off in life, my re-grouping may be slow, but the miracle is that the psychic life continues, and no matter how long I have been kept down, my essence rises above where I have gone to ground, and sings its way up again. The wrongs done are apprehended and my psyche begins restoration. The life force continues.' [From "Women Who Run With the Wolves" by Clarissa Pinkola Estes, Ph.D.]

As I write this I am getting my surroundings back, and improved, getting new windows and divesting myself of the trappings left behind by my 'other' half as it was.
Last night I got rid of the train platforms ringing the outside of the house, I hired Raoul to help with this, perfect synchronicity as he also helped Gordon construct it. Full circle.
The final bit of track was removed from the platforms in the garage. For this, another production directed by Gordon.
He hired a small car in Vegas and got Ray to come from San Francisco to drive him to L.A.as I said earlier, he also got Jeff Ross, leader of the backing band for Peter & Gordon, The Knuckleheads to show up, why we still haven't figured out. Moral support or something.
They pried it all up, filled the tiny car with what they could fit, some of his books and so forth. He was off again. I said "What no kiss goodbye?" He refused.

The train platform and cat walk Gordon built in front of the house

****

I have been doing a lot of soul-searching, not agonizing over anything now, just being able to think some things through that I had noticed on my re-emergence into my world from the desperation, loss and despair I was in after the total upheavals of the past couple of years.
First the dissolution of my marriage then, the illness and subsequent death of Sun, and before all that the loss of my mother. It has been a time of big changes in a life that doesn't like changes much.

****

My scattered perseverance of writing again has brought
me back, some six months from the last entry. It is now
near the end of October. The clocks will be going back an
hour next week, the Santa Ana's are blowing and the
temperatures are in the 90s and very dry.
Last week were the wildfires in the northwest Valley's

**.

In August it seemed with the knowledge of Gerry & The
Pacemaker's and Peter & Gordon playing a free concert on
the Santa Monica Pier, that it might be a fun day; get back
to a normal friendship perhaps. A whole crowd of friends
and I went down to a beautiful day at the beach.
I had brought some of Gordon's mail. It was just going to
be a normal day as far as I was concerned, no trouble, just
fun.
We all got there early to get seats up front, Don Adey,
Mark Kline, Dory & Linda, Alisa, Roxy, Bob & Lily and
Sharmayne. David and Melissa Wall showed up and a few
of us went to one of the restaurants on the Pier for a bite to
eat. Back at the stage, Peter (Asher) spotted me and Jeff
Ross, the keyboard player, we said a quick hello and both
came down to kiss my cheek and shoot the breeze.
When Gordon arrived he hid himself away. He had Jen
with him, his new wife, though he left her alone guarded
over by Kathy Holland.
Kathy had a bug up her ass from the start and was looking
to make trouble for and with me. I gave her a wide berth.
The show was quite good, Gordon seemed a bit off health
wise, he had gained too much weight, bloat, he always

retained water, it is bad for his heart and he would take diuretics before shows when he had them. His face looked fallen on one side, and he bent over in pain when he tried to 'sing out' on "Let It Be Me", he didn't look at all happy with the way things were turning out for him in his personal life, it wasn't his own, or it would seem. The night wore on and the show ended.

A nice anecdote to it all was when Peter & Gordon were singing "500 Miles" Joan Baez came up and sang with them, kissed Gordon on the cheek and gracefully left the stage.

On the Santa Monica Pier, with Don Adey

When we were all leaving, Kathy started running her mouth about all sorts of unnecessary nonsense, as we passed. Kathy, it would seem had always had a problem with me, she was jealous and wanted Gordon to be hers exclusively. Oh, not sexually, not as his girlfriend, but she was bossy and orchestrated Gordon's life to what she figured it should be, and it didn't include me.

She started saying some hurtful things, making fun of the stiff way I used to be forced to walk before I got my hips replaced, the topper was when she told me, with a smirk, that it was about time my horse had died. After all, whenever she had Gordon where she wanted him, I always had to drag him away to take care of Sun.

She was looking for a fight, something to go back and tell Gordon about that would make him stay displeased with me.

As she kept getting closer and closer, right up in my face, taunting me, I took a step back to regain my balance and reached out to steady myself and ended up slapping her across her spiteful face, turned on my heel and started walking back to my car and next thing I knew she had come up behind me and grabbed onto my hair, literally swinging on it with all her might!

She knows from my past physical disabilities that I must not fall. Hip replacements don't take kindly to that sort of treatment, so she swung and pulled on my hair till I crumpled to the rough and uneven Boardwalk, landing hard on my back. Where she proceeded to sit on me and shout "Police! Police!"

She then decided to try and get me arrested for attacking her!

I told the police the situation. I was the ex-wife and Kathy the Fan Club president, they believed me, and the truth. They were obliged to file the report and months later I went to see the Santa Monica City Attorney, explained again, and had a witness with me, Bob Granite.

When I got to the D.A.'s office in Santa Monica, I went in and told my story to David Fairweather, the D.A.

As it was, the whole thing was due to be off the books and just 'go away' in a few months so I agreed no contact between Kathy and I was ever necessary and it went away.

As it so conveniently happened, David was a very good friend of Arthur Lee and Love, he asked if I knew Arthur's widow Diane and I did, we chatted, seems he had toured with Arthur and Baby Lemonade. Old home week!

We now see each other at gigs and around town socially and we attended David's 60th birthday party, but I get ahead of myself.

Johnny & I with David Fairweather at David's 60th

I thought about suing Kathy as my back was bad after those contortions she put me through, but it is all too much trouble for too little reward in the end. I saw what happened, my friends saw what happened, and if a couple of other people who wanted to join me there had been able to show up there might have been some royal ass-kicking going on!

Rumbling at our ages is amazing!

I now feel the gloves are off and I have no business waiting on Gordon to come and collect his things, out they go, I got rid of the roll top desk Kathy had dumped on us when she and Terry moved to Vegas, got a new sofa, and moved Gordon's aura out of here. The persistence of memory!

My neighbour presented me with a great large screen TV, as he and his wife had gotten a newer one. It is new and improved around here.

****

I have already touched on the high school reunion from Hollywood Professional School. It was interesting, as I remembered very few of the people and very little about school. I didn't like school and I know why, some of the people are great. Jodie and Adrienne and Bob and Marilyn, Russell and a few others, but the rest?

Writing on their site. Oh my! Same bad memories of the school-yard cruelty and jealousies are still going strong. I was suspended from making posts on their site in the end. It is certainly a way to free up time to write more important missives.

I found out some funny incidents from Russ Haney. When I crashed that 1955 Plymouth on my way to El Monte Legion Stadium in April 1966, going to see Gordon, Russ was my ride to school for a while. He also took me to some parties, school parties mostly.

One he took me to was at the house of another classmate, Michael Lloyd; I hear he became a music producer for film music placement. Apparently he was rather displeased with me as I wanted to go get some weed. Russ took me and I was persona none gratis at his festivities, but it was good weed. Then a time after that, I had procured about a kilo for Russ and he had band practice so couldn't come for it, so he sent his room-mate Mickey Rooney Jr. and I had put it in the mailbox down at the road at my parents place. Glad he came and got it or the postman would have had a nice find the following day!

Nice trying to piece together memories from school after all.

With Russ Haney at the HPS reunion

Clearing out the dead wood is an interesting process. I find if I just let go of what I thought I needed, I don't miss it after a while.

I miss Sun. That is the only constant.

The shallow relationships and small talk, the user people, the opportunists. That is not missed at all.

Whoever I have drifted away from, I really didn't need any more.

Once a relationship has served its purpose, both good and bad, it is OK for it to be done with it. Healthier for all.

Things and people come in and go out of our lives. They serve a purpose for the both of you for a time, but trying to hang onto the original relationship is futile and counter-productive.

I have started a meditation practice. It is called Holosync, from Centerpointe. It utilizes sounds to achieve the same brain wave patterns Yogis take years in achieving through deep meditation. So, as the sun goes down I put on stereo headphones and listen to these subliminal sounds and get a great feeling of peace and relaxation. Transcendental Meditation without years of practice.

I still have my health matters, I have my epidurals and nerve blocks when needed. Recently I had to have an MRI on my brain, from a bang on the head over the spot where I messed all those nerves up in 1978. But I feel stronger than I did and more competent.

The economy of the world has gone down the shitter these past months, I am not alone in my tough times, I manage with caution.

I have always been able to live more simply alone than others are now having to do. Tightened my belt a long time ago and now everyone else is having to learn to live somewhat within their means. Like I had been in rehearsal for times like this all my life. An interesting object lesson for the world.

From that day on the Pier, I began to move on. Again.

****

Some time has now passed since last writing this. It is now a new decade in the new millennium.

The universe was obviously not done with me yet. Another summer ended and the cycle of death and rebirth came round again.

I would hear news about Gordon from time-to-time. He was working some and now lived in Connecticut somewhere.

I got an e mail of a newspaper article, Gordon had been arrested after running his rent-a-car into a wall, he was drunk, over three times the legal limit, same old song.

It was not my problem as a wife, it was not my problem at all, but I still felt so terribly sorry for him. I had tried, he hadn't. This was March of 2009.

I found out, subsequently, that Elizabeth, Gordon's mother, had died in February, of that same year, that explained a lot.

Gordon was always finding an excuse to binge drink when anything happened to anybody, not just in his own family, so I had always dreaded the time when Elizabeth would pass away. She was in her 90s and I can imagine his state-of-mind when it finally happened.

Spring turned to summer and my health and attitude had improved greatly. I was coming to terms with the way the changes in my life had affected me.

One early afternoon, the phone rang and it was Don Butler, of Working Class Hero. He was cautious and asked how was I doing? Well, I was fine, and how were he and Bonny?

"Oh, you haven't heard." Was all he said. I told him "out with it" and he had the difficult duty of telling me, the ex-wife, that my husband had passed away.

A shock, but no surprise. It took me a minute or two to process this, after all, I had just been awoken by the call.

I had told Gordon, just before he went away that November 7th 2006 that I could not watch him die. He would need to get himself together, stop smoking and drinking, the doctors had just told him the same a week or so before he left. He would need to do this, or leave.

He chose to leave and I feel he must have sobered up once or twice after that, just wondering what in the hell he had done, he had gone past the point of no return, as far as me, and living here in California that is.

What, indeed, had he done?

Gordon insisted on doing everything he could to destroy himself, but he was scared to actually die from it, he compounded this by making it all worse, the eternal struggle for staying in a haze, finally, it just did him in.

Poor man, must have felt he had nowhere to go but down.

This was the 17th July 2009. Gordon Waller was

dead at 64. He had only just had his birthday on the 4th June.

I made the obligatory telephone calls, the family, his sisters Anne and Diana, his daughters Phillippa and Natalie, his grand-daughter Tyla; it seems they had been 'awarded' as Gordon's in the divorce and none but Annie spoke to me, and it was awkward. She told me then that their mother had passed away in February and Gordon had not sobered up much since, he lasted five months, and followed his mum out of this world.

There was to be a service, or something in Connecticut, I, of course, was not on that guest list. I don't think I would have gone regardless.

I know not what happened. I called the hospital where he died, cardiac arrest, and no one had even sent the body to a funeral home all that week-end. He died on a Thursday, it wasn't till the following Monday anyone even got to his body. The daughters wanted to see him apparently, and after their desperate efforts at the Wm. Backus Hospital in Norwich, CT. It was not, I should imagine, a pretty sight. I would rather remember him in better days.

He had always told me he wanted to be scattered at sea, whether this happened or not, I do not know. I hope he found some peace is all.

I have a death certificate here, it says atherosclerotic cardiovascular disease; his poor heart couldn't take the beating of extraneous substances nor the pain of losing in love once again. It was hard to love Gordon. Or rather, it was easy to love him, just very hard to like him sometimes.

43

He still never came for the rest of his things. I still haven't gotten around to moving them out of sight, there is just so much it is over-whelming. Luckily there is plenty of space around here and it can all be avoided, perhaps too easily.

It is, in retrospect, such a shame that he did what he did at the end. Leaving like he did, hurt and angry and drunk, hoping to find acceptance for his behaviour from this new woman, a woman who will let him kill himself daily and not help. Subsequently I have found out that the U-Haul I chased with Ray behind the wheel of all Gordon's possessions, his guitars especially, were put into a storage facility, the expensive items were later removed by Jen and she just disappeared. So his daughters how have nothing, whereas they would have had their father's things if they had been left with me. I even had a notice from his Barclay's account in England, I told them his new wife's contact information, along with the death certificate and so forth. A few weeks later, they sent me a cheque of about £465, seems they had tried to find this Jen Chowdry, to no avail and I was the widow for all intents and purposes. Actually, truth be told, she was never legally married to Gordon as I never signed the divorce papers. I had never been served after all. The server just illegally stuffed them in the mailbox. Unknown to everyone, Gordon was also very possibly, a bigamist, albeit unknowingly.

Gordon Waller

****

The outpouring of love from our friends was tremendous.
I had more flowers and cards and calls and e mails, and of
course, the news services.
I may have been the ex-wife, but I was now 'The Widow'.
He had, after all, only married Jen in a fit of pique a short 3

months before. And he had only been away for 16 months in all.

Michael Mitchell called from San Francisco and said we should have a Wake. He came down and we started inviting. The house on the 25th July was filled with all the people close to me, to him, to us. Gordon and I were still "Gordon & Georgie", ironic really considering the past 16 months.

At the wake: Nancy Van Iderstine, me, Don Butler, and Alisa Curran.

Don Adey and Don Butler

Music was played, videos were watched. Many of the guests, Annette Pitre, J.P.'s wife in particular, reported to me that Gordon was there, while she smoked outside, she saw him on the outside train platform or just out in his garage having a ciggie, and probably a drink as well! And Annette died of lung cancer just a few months later.

Dallas Hodge, of Canned Heat with Annette and John Pitre

It was closure and though the Kathy Holland faction may have tried to erase me from Gordon's life, it was not to be so.

Another ending. Life does continue, and in a way I was now free from wondering what was up with Gordon, he was still affecting my life after he left, now, not more than memories of him now and again.

Tom MacLear

There were events, Tom MacLear, playing with Dallas Hodge, from Canned Heat, dedicated a set to Gordon at Cozy's night club in Sherman Oaks. John Walker and his wife Cynthia showed up, they had been to Connecticut I believe. Other concerts have been bandied about in the planning stages, but getting all musicians together for such an event is difficult as tour schedules intervene. It is all for the living at this point, not really a memorial as such. Michael went back to San Francisco and within a day or two called to ask if he could come back and no sooner had he gotten home that he and his wife Kay, decided to divorce.

Another full circle, Michael, my friend for 45 years is now residing in my spare room.

What goes around does surely come around again.

Cynthia and John Walker (Maus) with Tom MacLear at Cozy's~

Michael and I at Cozy's 10th July 2009

Don Adey, Tom MacLear and I at Cozy'

Usual suspects: Skip, Don. Dallas and Tom (and two)

****

Now, another year has passed, we are coming up on the
one year's anniversary of Gordon's passing, the third for
Sun's departure.
Peter Asher, Gordon's daughters Phillippa and Natalie, his
first wife Gay and some musician friends of Gordon's and
mine over the years had a memorial concert at the
Cannery Hotel in Las Vegas the end of May.
I was at Gordon's and my timeshare in Carlsbad.
Vegas was not my place to be anyway. Gay and her and
Gordon's daughters had to have their own closure. I am
grateful for Peter and the band, also Ian Whitcomb, Denny

Laine, Spencer Davis and John Walker as well as Sonny Curtis and others came together for a final send-off.

 I got my torn ACL, which had been done by Sun's errant hoof some eleven years ago, repaired this past month, June 2010, and it is healing nicely. The weather has turned hot, at last and life moves along; it is now July 2010.
The wildfires of last year proved beneficial, not to the poor folks who were displaced by it, but soot and smoke damage afforded me a nice sum from the insurance company.
There's that universe helping out again!

****

The time flew, and while writing on My Space one evening I saw a message from a familiar name out of my past. Johnny Echols from Love. Hadn't seen or spoken to him since about 1968!

Johnny Echols back in the day with his double-neck…

Johnny had re-formed Love after Arthur's death with their backing band Baby Lemonade as Love revisited and they were going to be playing down in Long Beach, did I want to come? Well, firstly, I marveled how he remembered me after all this time, no surprise, I remembered him too. Johnny was living in Sedona, Arizona.
The night of the show came around and I woke with a pinched sciatic nerve and couldn't make it. Oh well, next time.
Luckily there was one, not too far off, in Long Beach again. I went to Alex's Bar in March 2011.
When we laid eyes on each other again it was like coming home. Just fell back into our old friendship. Magic!

There was another gig in Sierra Madre a couple of months later.

Johnny Echols and I with Nick Koff at our first re-meeting

Johnny was staying at Vince's house in Pacific Palisades, and one night I was going to see Tim Piper's production of John Lennon's retrospective "Just Imagine" so I asked Johnny and Vince along with Cathy Senogles, and we went down to Wilshire Blvd. and the Hayworth Theatre, it was already October.

The show was, as usual fantastic. Imagine John Lennon gets to come back to earth and give one last concert. Very well done, Tim Piper and his brother Greg along with

Morely Bartnoff and Don's Butler and Poncher put on a great show.

Just Imagine cast: l-r Don Butler, friend, Tim Piper, me and Johnny, Greg Piper and Morley Bartnoff

It was like a first date. Holding hands and going to the theatre. We got back here to the house and sat, talked and had a smoke, Cathy had to get back home and Vince was prepared to leave without Johnny, but he declined and we met up at a later time.

Johnny came over for dinner and a movie where we talked and talked and laughed, when it came time for bed, it only seemed natural to stay.

After a bit we said something like" well, do you want to give it a try?" No bullshit, just honesty and always remain

friends, no matter what the future may hold? We both decided it was a good idea and we have been nearly inseparable since. It is now February of 2018..
To find love, real love, at 60 is amazing.
I have come to realise what love is really all about and that is good. Johnny seems to feel the same and we are doing our things together.

Johnny & I at the Hayworth for Just Imagine

A funny segue or two must be inserted here. One of my
favourite things is to find degrees of separation and circles
within circles.

For this we travel back to 2007, or further.

When Gordon disappeared I went on his computer hoping to find a clue, no one had heard from him. I found messages between Gordon and a Nancy Bragin. Nothing more that flirty exchanges. So, I wrote to her and just asked what she had to do with my husband, nothing accusatory. I got a reply, though I wasn't expecting one. Nancy, as it turned out was doing a documentary on Peter & Gordon and had been in touch with both of them getting interviews, she also went to a gig in Toronto and did interviews there, and she had gotten Gordon a book deal. Gordon had mentioned this in anger as he was preparing himself to leave, that he was getting a hefty advance and he was giving it all to Jen. When I found the publishers address I wrote to them and showed them a picture of him lying on the kitchen floor with a bloody nose from falling, oh, he had also pissed himself, it was taken by his sponsor to show him later...well, I quashed the book deal, but hell hath no fury like a woman scorned, and all that!

But back to the synchronicity of Nancy, Vince and Johnny...When Nancy had explained to me that she should have felt insulted at my e mail, as she had been married a long time and had a grown son, but I didn't know that, so we started corresponding and became very good friends, considering that she lives in Philadelphia and I California. So when another documentary Nancy worked on "The Wages of Spin", an expose of the nefarious business practices of Dick Clark.,was being screened at U.C.L.A. and Nancy came out and stayed with me here.

Michael Mitchell and Mark Kline came along, and another acquaintance of Nancy's Vince Flaherty. The same Vince whose house Johnny stayed at when in L.A.

Now, about 5 years into our relationship, I learn from Johnny that Vince had mentioned meeting me on this occasion to Johnny when he got home, so the seeds were sown.

I am amazed and so very relieved every day to find I have a strong intelligent and like-minded person to be with. And through a circuitous route of people we were first made aware of then brought ourselves together again.

Thom, Nancy Bragin, myself Vince and a Ken with friend

****

After the nightmare of Gordon, going on a binge both times I was recuperating from hip surgeries, Johnny was perfect.

When I had to get my left knee replaced, Johnny was there, constantly, we shared my morphine and watched the entire series of "Breaking Bad", and then I was up and about again, dancing at The Trip in Santa Monica a month later, dancing to Nick Koff's band Bunnynose and later at a party at Vince's estate while Johnny and Don Adey played.

3/30/2014

Dancing on my new knee at Vince's party a month after replacement

Warwick Rose, my dear friend from back in the day in London has wonderful soiree's at his house in Bell Canyon, permanently set up to jam, musicians practically queue up to play music, eat, drink and be merry till the wee hours.

With Brian Chatton, keyboards for Yes, and Laurie Shoshan at Warwick's

Regulars at the jam are always Albert Lee and some good session people, Guitar Shorty turned up a couple of times. Great nights.

With Warwick Rose, Johnny Echols and Albert Lee

Warwick Rose and I

John York plays monthly at the Coffee Gallery Backstage in Alta Dena, CA.

For a great retrospective in Byrd's, Dylan, the Band and others, including material written by John and Gene Clark, Billy Darnell, who plays lead, along with Chad Watson on bass make up the Jangle Bros. formerly Byrd's and Beyond till McGuinn asked John to change it as promoters were messing up and putting Jim (aka Roger)'s face on the ads. John was also touring the world with Barry McGuire doing "Trippin' the Sixties". Fantastic look back through chatting and songs. Barry retired earlier this year and you can only catch the show on You Tube.

Barry Maguire and I

Johnny and I with John and Sumi York

* *

Life is never full of sweetness and light all of the time, and frankly, without lows how do you recognize the highs?

The cycle of life and death happens all through our lives, but the amount of friends who have shuffled off this mortal coil is unprecedented when not in war time. Many of us had way too much fun and were careless with our bodies' way too long. I still dabble in 'shrooms on occasion and smoke pot daily, but the hard substances no longer find a place in my recreation.

Happily, many you would not have thought to have lasted have not only prevailed but come out stronger to enjoy their 70's and hopefully beyond.

The lifespan of our pets is unfortunately too short. The little Miniature Pinscher, Caesar, Gordon brought home one night was only 9.

One weekend he had a terrific thirst, I mean, like licked the walls of the shower for water. Johnny and I got him to the vet to find he had diabetes, un-known to us or the vet in previous visits. His sugar was well over 3000 and that is not good. We left him over night and returned the following day, he was quiet, but his sugar was down and we left him another day, the following morning Dr. Jimerson called to say to get down there quickly, Caesar had had a heart attack. We rushed down he was resting in an oxygen infused cage, he looked up when we came in a barked, I opened the door and pet him and spoke to him softly and he closed his eyes and was gone. Poor little guy.

Saying good-bye to Caesar

Then Smudge, my kitten from 2001 started getting skinny just after her 15th birthday. Thus began another round of fluids at the vet's and that was all that we could do. She had a slight mass in her liver, but was in no pain, so for the next few weeks, she lingered, getting weaker and weaker, but happy in her surroundings. On the morning of the 24th June she was laying on her cushion under the window where she would sit and look out, stiff. She now lays under the earth in a flower bed she would watch the sun go down at night from.

Smudge

Bobby Jameson had a horrific time, first his mother, Troy had a stroke, she was 96, while she was in hospital his brother Bill who was a schizophrenic, went into a state where he just curled up and wouldn't eat, Bobby had ordeals with the hospital and rest home personnel, finally getting them both in the same hospital. First Bill died, then about a month later Troy passed. Bobby had untreated headaches for years, and a week after his 70th birthday in April, he died of an aneurysm in May.

He was never a happy camper, he too should have found peace and not let himself be consumed by others when he needed help himself. But it seems it was a family affair.

Bobby, Troy and Bill Jameson

In July of 2010 Michael came in and woke me. Harvey, who had for the past 18 years always came up and made himself coffee and toast, didn't. We went down the back stairs and I peeked in his window, Harvey was sitting on the floor, with his face down on the bed, I was barefoot, so Michael went in and felt for a pulse and there wasn't one. Harvey was gone and I called the police and the coroner to deal with the remains. Harvey had no relatives, but fortunately was a vet and so the VA handled everything.

The cat I had brought home for him, Sooty, went feral for a couple of months, now he is a fat housecat.

Harvey Gardner, Iron Eyes Cody me and Willie Nelson

A few were lost to cancer. Teddy Garcia, from the Forge days, dance partner for all the line dancing and two-stepping died of kidney cancer, Kim Fowley, from days gone by, brought into my circle once more by a set of circumstances involving another friend, Kara,

Kim Fowley and I at Amoeba Records for 'Where the Action Is boxed set release

succumbed to liver cancer, and sadly my old friend Mark Kline, after bouts with prostate cancer and lymphoma finally couldn't beat cancer of the liver. I was saddened that I found out after his passing and his daughter Kayla tried to find me as Mark wanted me to visit him in hospital, had I known, I would have gone to see him one last time, but it was not to be and now, since they were offered to friends at the memorial, Johnny has a great selection of his expressive T-shirts, and I also got his collection of Reggae and African music CD's. His tastes live on! We also lost Jackie Lomax, and the Cat & Fiddle was bought and closed. Another transitioning.

At the Cat & Fiddle for Jackie Lomax' memorial. With Jimmi Mayweather, Don Adey and Johnny Echols

Myself with Mark and Kayla Kline at my mother's memorial Nov. 2007

The photographer of so many Sixties artists, Herbie Worthington died and his memorial was held at El

Coyote Mexican Restaurant in Beverly Hills. Well attended by friends it was a warm event.

Herbie Worthignton's memorial at El Coyote with Leon Hendrix and Rae Rae and Riley Racer and others

****

Another unfortunate incident happened a couple of years ago.

Remember the guy at the reunion? Bob Granite? When Johnny was off getting some of his belongings in Arizona, Bob calls one day to ask if I knew anyone who wanted a good new car for a great price. Probate cars were being sold off and he had a list of some very nice vehicles, one, the 2011 Prius for $9000, remember it was 2012, sounded good, so I said I would want to see it. He was up here in a flash to collect the down payment to keep it. I gave him a cheque for $5000. He said he would call when I could go to Van Nuys court where they were being stored. In the meantime he called to ask if I wanted to make enough money back that the Prius would be free, so I said "sure and gave him another $5000 then he would share the cost on two of the other high end cars, which we would flip. Meanwhile Johnny has been on the phone and when I tell him he jumped back in the car and drove back to L.A. from Sedona post haste, told me it was too good to be true, sort of thing, oh had I but listened. He managed to get another couple of thousand from me, each day calling to tell us the time to meet the lawyers there. Then another call to push it back, and back and back. This, believe it or not went on for a couple of months, every day, the morning call the appointment, pushed back periodically over the day till it was after 4pm and the courts were closed, then the lawyers son was in a motorcycle accident, then he died, lawyers had to go the San Francisco to get his things, bury him, etc. He sounded so believable, and as his mother had been my mother's agent and we had gone to school together...though I had no memory. I told myself, and Johnny all these salient points which meant nothing at all. I was down about $17,000 by this point as he had given me two cheques back and I deposited them and they bounced after I had paid bills and so forth!

We went to the police, nothing, called major crime, has to be over $350,000. I even asked Judge Judy! No help is available.

But, the sheer gall to tell all those tales, about a lawyer's son's dying and so forth, just devious.

I should have listened to Johnny and not given him any money without seeing the cars, there were no cars either, by the way.

He has also ripped off a few others, some I know, like Marylin Gambill and Larry Stuppy from Hollywood Professional School. Lily finally figured out what Bob was doing and was trying to get a class action against Bob, but I can't afford a lawyer for what would, no doubt, be a futile endeavour.

****

There is so much still happening, I can't see why to grow old. The Love-In I started up again in 2011 has been blossoming year-after-year. We grow in reputation and size every year. We had two during a Blue Moon one year, it was also the day Scott McKenzie died, we had invited him, I had known he was ill, but not that ill. A tree up in the park cracked and broke right at the time of death, like he wished he could have been there.

There was a great memorial for him held at the Whisky where people like Michelle Phillips, Owen Elliot-Kugle (Mama Cass's daughter), Barry McGuire, John York and many more got to relive his life and music along with all his friends.

Outside the Whisky with the plaque mentioning Love

Michelle Phillips, and I and Sumi York at the Whiskey

Johnny's reflection in Scott Mackenzie's guitar

At Scott's memorial with Owen Elliot-Kugle (Mama Cass' daughter)

The arrangement with Michael Mitchell living here didn't work out, we are old friends but cannot be around each other constantly like that. We are friends and he has stayed here with Johnny and me whilst retrieving some of his belongings. He went to live at Ray's in San Francisco which is another circle, and for 5 years all has been OK, he had colon cancer and two hips replaced, so we can understand each other better. But now, the constant Gemini is moving on again to Sacramento this time.

Another fun evening was the Wild Honey Benefit for Autism at the Alex Theatre here in Glendale. Saw many friends performing the Beatles White Album. Even friend Keith Allison was there.

Johnny and I with Keith Allison at the Alex Theatre

The Who, on their massive 50 years in the biz tour of the world had to put the LA gig, along with the rest, on hold till the spring as Roger contracted Meningitis and needs to rest till May. I have our passes. So will be at the Staples Centre on the 25th. Get well soon Rog!

Roger Daltrey and I at the Nokia Theatre

Johnny and Love revisited have been playing now and again, and we are scheduled to go over to the U.K. June 2016 for a two –week tour. Should be fun to see the old place again. Different without mum over there, but another destination through that door will do me good too.

If it all works out well, there are talks in the works for a European tour and then Australia and Japan.

Friends have never given up on the dream of fronting, or playing in a band, no matter what their ages.

Don Adey has a regular gig at Barone's restaurant, Nick Koff plays all around town as Bunnynose, and each show is a gathering of us rag-taggle hippies. Keeps us all young.

Johnny and I with Nick Koff aka Bunnynose

The Happy Together Tours have been fun. With The Turtles, Mark Lindsay, Chuck Negron, Gary Lewis and many from Top 40 radio to try to remember

With Marc Lindsay of Paul Revere and the Raiders

With Howard Kaylan of the Turtles

Johnny & I with Chuck Negron of Three Dog Night

With saxophonist extraordinaire John Altman @ Viva

Johnny and I at the Love exhibit, Grammy Museum

Johnny and I with Mark Volman of the Turtles

We have become interesting to succeeding generations, and a look into the past for those of our ages.

I have done interviews; both for "In My Life, So Far..." and for documentaries of other's, whose projects I was involved in.

There is The Who's "'Can You See the Real Me?' The Making of Quadrophenia", of which I was contacted for my input. It is now available on You Tube and I believe I start in Pt 4.

My friend Jodie Carn from Hollywood Professional does an interview show, "Jodie in Malibu". The two part interview is also available on You Tube.

During our interview for "Jodie in Malibu"; Jodie Carn

Johnny and I both were interviewed for Gerry Gallagher's radio show broadcast weekly from the Four Season's Hotel in Calabasas, and joined the festivities in subsequent Thursdays till they took a break to re-format.

Our friend Tina Malave from Channel 7's Eye On L.A. won an Emmy for her documentary on the music "Legends of Laurel Canyon", which Johnny participated in; Cool that we were once again in the house on Love St, as Jim Morrison's house, where he and Pamela Courson lived has been re done after a fire and Matt King kindly opened his home to us for the viewing. And another viewing of the show at the home of Alison Martino.

Another documentary "Pushin' Too Hard" about The Seed's late Sky Saxon was picking Johnny's brain for insight, and he gave the funniest reply of the whole film!

With Diane Lee, Kara Wright-Fowley and Tina Malave

Johnny and I being interviewed by Gerry Gallagher

With Johnny and Dave Perlman at a Sapphire Club dinner

Happy at last! Johnny and I on my 65th birthday at The Trip

Jodie Carn and I

****

I have found my place again, one might say. I seem to have kept testing the waters of many different lifestyles, we all do, or should. Like all children, we distance ourselves from the lives of our parents, trying to find the niche where we belong, where we are most comfortable. Only to come full circle and settle into a lifestyle similar to theirs' in many cases.

I was fortunate to have had the parents I did, who now, looking back on it, were trying to fit into the role of parents after being involved in the crazy days of Hollywood and the characters that inhabited it.

I have had many incarnations, of lifestyles; and although I have always dealt with whatever situation I found myself in, and seemingly fit in enough to get whatever done with the people I have been working with, I never felt like I was a true part of those situations. Only among the seeming outcasts and differently abled have I found total honesty and comfort. So the trying to distance myself from parental influence and control has only come full circle and I remind myself of them more and more each day. The social situations, and even the types of people they knew, I now know their counterparts.

From the very early days, I was treated differently somehow. Just being an only child with older parents who liked to party; the other parents were often doubtful to let their kids play with me.

My parents were world travelers and in show business, and had had many relationships, oh, and mum had been married twice before my father.

Dad built a bar room in part of the old barn/garage of our house on Orion Ave. The idea that they served alcohol around children, well, it was just too much for many of the puritanical parents of the 1950's, we didn't drink it!

Then later on, when I was modelling and missed a lot of school; dressed against the school dress code, was sent home or required to stay in the Girls Vice Principals office because my skirt was too short or some other non-scholastic nonsense. I went from school to school and finally ended up my schooling at Hollywood Professional School. All theatrical kids, but even there, I drifted away from my classmates and searched the more exciting venues for mental and physical stimulation.

Being able to go back to London at nineteen broadened my outlook and I once again found myself trying out different strata's of society. Always seeking for that which was different. The high society of Europe, all the being subjected to the polite society of the Rothschild's at a resort my god father Herbie Newmark took me to in Switzerland, luxurious but mentally vapid, the Al-Fayad's lavishing gifts and shopping trips in Milan and Genoa were not as much fun as staying in London and dropping acid with my friends.

My parents went to clubs, Ciro's, Mocambo, Trocadero, Coconut Grove, Cotton Club, 21, Les Ambassadeur and others, and I had Ciro's as well as Bido Lito's and the Whisky, Rainbow, The Trip, Kaleidoscope, The Speakeasy and Tramp. Where the poets and minstrels, madmen and drunkards, opium eaters and so forth congregated. Here I felt in my milieu.

I had times where I had to take mundane jobs, not careers, dad had to take day jobs between theatrical endeavours, and mum tried a job at Harrods once that lasted about 3 hours when she objected being told what to do by her manager who was younger than I at the time.

I see now that trying to fit in doesn't always work. You don't have to argue with people to know you just have nothing in common. But I couldn't live like that and am so very glad I have attracted to me people of like minds and temperaments. No matter what their ages. We have friends in their 70's and 80's as well as in their 30's, we all learn from each other. I still have a friend in his nineties. He never got old either.

Love In at the Merry-Go-Round in Griffith Park 2015

The friends, old and new, have just drifted together, especially with social media. We have re-found those thought lost forever, as well as catching up with friends we missed the first time around. The Love Ins' have attracted more and more every year. Our bodies may not move as smoothly as we once did, but the attitudes and like minds have gathered the tribes together once again. We have no peer pressure and jealousies that youth is fraught with and can sit together and make music in a pleasant haze of legal medical marijuana!

Riding the Carousel on 'shrooms 2014

My close circle are people of varied interests, but all done with the free spirit of discovery and tweaking the norm to be the way we wanted as teenagers. Hippies still!

At The Trip in Santa Monica for Love and Bunnynose l-r
Mo, Craig Clairbourne, Johnny and I, Riley Racer,
Annette Ferrel, Mindi Sparks and Elaine Boucher

The bands of the Sixties and Seventies are still touring,
with the same personnel or adequate replacements for
the ones no longer with us.

Johnny and Love revisited have been playing again,
locally and in San Diego, and we are scheduled to go
over to the U.K. June 2016 for a two–week tour.

Should be fun to see the old place again. Different
without mum over there, but another destination
through that door will do me good too.

If it all works out well, there are talks in the works for a European tour and then Australia and Japan.

Gathering for the Love revisited gig at the El Cid; John and Joy Bonehill, Annette Ferrel, Kara Wright-Foley, myself and Gretchen.

Kara Wright-Fowley arranged a great thing for Johnny and Love. Every year there are certain acts of the past who get giant oversized guitars with their names. They are displayed along the Sunset Strip and then auctioned off for charity, to keep music in the schools. When Love got theirs, it was displayed over the door at the Whisky. The launch party at the Jaguar dealership on Sunset was a fun event, Robbie Krieger of the Doors came by to offer his congratulations.

97

At the Love guitar unveiling, l-r Robbie Krieger, Diane Lee, (Arthur's widow) Kara Wright-Fowley, (Kim's widow), myself (Gordon's widow...) my love Johnny Echols and Ronni Harran-Melon.

Went to the annual anniversary party at the Rainbow, 43rd this year!! Mario, at 91 is still holding court and running the show. Fabulous man. New nose and all!

At the Rainbow's 43rd anniversary party with Mario Maglieri.

Johnny & I at The Rainbow's 43rd

The Grammy Museum in Downtown Los Angeles had their opening exhibit on, of course, Laurel Canyon in the Sixties. Love had an exhibit of their own, it was very cool. Here are some pics of the day.

The Laurel Canyon Exhibit at the Grammy Museum

With Rodney Bingenheimer at the Grammy Museum & Love Exhibit

Johnny with the guitar for Forever Changes

with Alison Martino at her home

With Donna and Micky Dolenz at the Canyon Country store on our way to the screening at Jim Morrison's old house.

With Randy Brooks at first Love In in 2011

All in all we are involved, together, for the rest of our lives. Having a ball.

****

It is strange, at 65 I feel no different, but for the physical problems of course, but mentally, I still have the silliness of youth, and except for knowing that time is now of the essence, or perhaps because of it, my life is fuller now than the days and years floundering between situations, trying to find a place to fit in comfortably.

Don't get me wrong, the floundering was educational and full of experiences I wouldn't trade for anything. Both good and bad; and in ways, especially the bad, as they were life lessons that helped me grow as an individual. I have only ever been able to really learn from experience; my own, not from others. Even from my parents, whose lives I see mine now paralleling, I just had to do it myself before I could see it was also their way. Just updated.

Live and learn holds very true, live and learn.

So, dear reader, I leave you with this idea: have fun, have humour, your lives are your own, don't let anyone change you if it is uncomfortable for you, respect yourself and the world around you, and realise nothing, even life and death is all that serious in the scheme of things, look after each other.

****

FIN

Ω